Encyclopedia Of Spiritual Development

Book Two

Pam Brittan

Encyclopaedia of Spiritual Development – Book Two

Encyclopedia of Spirit original copyright Pam Brittan 2013

Website: www.spiritenergyuk.co.uk

Email: pambrittan@spiritenergyuk.co.uk

Pam Brittan

All rights reserved.

Encyclopaedia of Spiritual Development – Book Two

DEDICATION

I dedicate this to all my family and friends and those who have supported be through my many years of working with Spirit.
Most of all I am humbled by the messages I have received from those in the Spirit World to enable me to collate this book for sale.

During my time serving Spirit I have met many wonderful people. I have very often been in awe of the experiences I have had and the pleasure it has given me to help those in need. It has been a devotion; it has been about giving time and making sacrifices but, doing the work with love and light.

No amount of teaching can give you that understanding it is only by doing the work, listening and not judging. It is about having wonderful encounters with people of like mind and feeling the joy of the work.

These encyclopedias' have given me the chance to amalgamate the knowledge I have gained and put it into precise easy words for the reader to understand.

Each step of this journey has to come from the heart but, most of all not from the expectation of what the ego wants. Put aside that thought; very few brilliant mediums go on to do stage tours and be famous, most just want to do the work in the best way they know how; if you work on this premise, then, dear reader, you will know you will succeed.

Love and light
Pam

CONTENTS

Chapter one: Using Tools

Chapter Two: Guides

Chapter Three: Angelic Forces

Chapter four: The soul the spirit, and the Higher Self.

Chapter One

Tools

We have talked about the Aura, the Chakras and the Brain all playing its part in the aspect of your psychic and spiritual abilities.

The Sensations felt during the effort of "tuning in" to another, all will have an important role to play even when you are using tools

The tools however could become a significant" prop" during readings enabling you to build your confidence to eventually "fly" without their use.

Tools are a valuable way of "Tuning In" to one another. You can use the literal meaning of the Tool i.e. using the book interpretation or use them in an inspirational way. Most people can use the book interpretation but when we use the tool in a psychic and spiritual level we are using other means of "tuning in".

Although we use the aura and the chakra energies the "tool" enables us to "tune" into that energy much quicker it also helps because the mind is focused on the "tool" rather than the person to whom we are trying to give information.

There are many "tools of the trade" Tarot Cards, Crystal Balls, Sand, Ribbons, Colour and aura cameras, Runes, and many more.

Some Clairvoyants will simply use playing cards and years ago lots of them used the tea leaves as a tool.

Looking into the Crystal Ball is using the art of Scrying which translates as peeping".

It is a practice that involves seeing things psychically in a vehicle usually for purposes of obtaining spiritual visions. In the first instance it was used less often for purposes of divination or fortune telling.

The most common media used are reflective, translucent, or luminescent substances such as: Crystals, Stones, Glass, Mirrors, Water, Fire and Smoke.

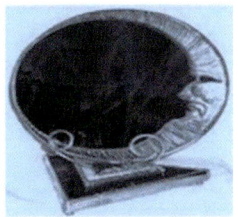

Scrying has been used in many cultures as a means of divining the past, present, or future. Depending on the culture and practice, the visions that come when one stares into the media are thought to come from the universe, the psychic mind, or the subconscious.

Method

The visions that scryers say they see may come from variations in the object used.

If water (hydromancy) is used, then the visions may come from the colour, ebb and flow, or ripples produced by pebbles dropped in a pool.

If a crystal ball is used, the visions may come from the tiny inclusions, web-like faults, or the cloudy glow within the ball under low light (e.g., candlelight).

One method of scrying using a crystal ball involves a self-induced trance. Initially, the tool used serves as a focus for the attention, removing unwanted thoughts from the mind in the same way as a mantra.

Once this stage is achieved, the scryer begins a free association with the perceived images suggested. The technique of deliberately looking for and declaring these initial images aloud, however trivial or irrelevant they may seem to the conscious mind, this is done with the intent of deepening the altered state of consciousness, in this state the scryer can "see" the images and "feel" the change in the vibration. .

One of the most famous scryers in history lived in the 16th century and was known as Nostradamus. He used a bowl of water or a "magic mirror" to "see" the future in it, while he was in trance.

In folklore

Divination rituals such as the one depicted on this early-20th-century Halloween greeting card,, where a woman stares into a mirror in a darkened room to catch a glimpse of the face of her future.

What are Sand Readings?

In a typical sand reading, the subject is told to place their hand on sand in a small box and it may also be told to draw a picture on the sand. Once the subject draws a picture, the psychic interprets the symbols on the sand based on the energies of the sand and the subject.

Most of the time, the psychic would draw a circle on the sand and ask the seeker to draw something without speaking a word. Then the psychic would interpret the drawing and tell the seeker about various solutions to his problems.

Native Americans were the pioneers in sand painting. They had dirt floors in their homes and they carried multi-coloured sand and painted the pictures on the floor. A psychic would then interpret these paintings based on the vibration of the painting and not by the mere pictures.

There are many schools of thought that we should only use these items as "Psychic" tools.

But as you begin your reading, because you often step into that altered state of consciousness during that time, often, a "Spirit" link will join you.

It is all about learning to recognise the different "energies" we are using . Then Trusting what is given to you – Remember you will use your imagination but let that inspire you!

Putting all the inspired pieces together to bring the message to the recipient.

There is another way of "tuning" in to another person's energy field and that is with the use of psychometry. Basically it is handling an object that belongs to the person who requires the sitting.

Whenever we handle an object we are laying down information about ourselves on that item. Because our bodies have given off that magnetic field it is like a recording on a CD or DVD. It will remain on that item as a recorded event.

Psychometry has its advantage in that it can bring lots of information from the person before you and the family, but if many people have handled that object the residue of their energy will also be on that item.

There is no right or wrong way, there is only THE WAY. Remember, to use RESPONSIBILITY at all times. Phrase your words very carefully and be diplomatic in your handling of the words you use. This phrase is repeated several times throughout this book. Your gift is wonderful but please be aware of the impact you make.

It is all about learning to recognise the different "energies" we are using .

Then Trusting what is given to you – Remember you will use your imagination but let that inspire you!

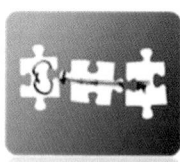

Practice with people of like mind using the cards or tools you have chosen. Look at them inspirationally and then use the book interpretation to see if you have accurately described what you have perceived.

I often say knowledge is power, but sometimes being naive and coming to something completely raw can add an excitement to a subject as well as a new perception to the tutor.

Often in the teaching we can learn; I never take it as read that I KNOW EVERYTHING because, dear reader, that would be very stupid of me!!!!!!

Even with all the experience during my many years of Mediumship I am still in awe of the messages, the synchronicity and the co-incidences that happen to enable us to be where we are, who we are with, and doing what we are doing.

No matter how old or experienced we think we have become, nothing can prepare us for the wonderful way Spirit can show us the way.

Oscar Wilde said "Life is far too important a thing ever to talk seriously about "

Live life and let Spirit guide you

Chapter Two

Guides

Spirit Guides are entities or beings that are currently in the spirit realms or dimensions. These are individuals, or groups of individuals, who have agreed with a person on the earth plane to act as their guide or guardian. Usually we enter into this agreement with at least one "primary guide" prior to being born into a physical body , this "guide" is our "doorkeeper"

These "primary guides" are often other members of our Soul Group

We can also call upon other "teachers" and "philosophers" when we are ready to receive their help. It is not uncommon to have two or more guides assisting us at a given moment. Many of the guides with which we work are beings who have lived on this earth plane at one time or another (or many lifetimes)

The "guides" that come to help us with special needs or learning experiences seem to be more evolved beings, or 'old souls' who are willingly sharing their expertise and expanded knowledge with those of us still working on our evolvement and enlightenment.

One of the primary purposes that Spirit Guides seem to have is the guiding and teaching of those under their care.

They agree to help us remember the lessons we set up for ourselves in this lifetime, and to instruct us with regards to those lessons. They can, and will, teach us as much as we want to learn. Their guidance, though, is of a very gentle nature. And they will not give us any more than we are ready to receive and capable of perceiving.

They're here to help us to learn, but they will not pressure us with the information unless they feel we are ready and willing. They'll counsel and help us see other perspectives, but they won't make the decisions for us; the choices are ours to make and to live with afterwards.

How many Spirit Guides can you have?

We actually have an unlimited number of Spirit Guides available to us. We can call 'special guides' to us to teach us specific lessons, and once those lessons have been learned, they will move on to help others. Also, as loved ones pass over, they can choose to act as additional Spirit Guides for us either 'full time' or on an 'as needed' basis.

Developing and Maintaining your Spirit Guide Contact

One of the fascinating things about working with Spirit Guides is that there is always something new to learn or to develop. Yet as answers come for questions, there is still more questions to ask!

Remember, some questions we already know, we have bought them with us and access to them will be in the aspect we call our higher consciousness.

When we start having the contact with our "doorkeeper" try to remember to keep a notebook or journal of the experiences you have had during this time

As your Guide becomes an ever-more familiar friend and mentor, they will give you guidance for your future spiritual and material development. Meditation is a very big factor to "tune in to the vibrational changes within your "Auric" field.

Recognising this change and acknowledging the difference by welcoming them in will start a dialogue with your 'doorkeeper'.

Finding the right place to meet with your "Spirit Guide" is practicing walking over the "RAINBOW BRIDGE" towards the Spirit World and internally asking them to draw close and meet you there.

This will mean practice, practice, practice however there will come a time when you will be able to speed this process up and harness the inner sense, to being joined by your power animal and your "doorkeeper"

In conscious co-creative channelling or mediumship, the guide can use only the vocabulary that is part of your knowledge, but the deeper the connection the more the "guide" will inspire you with "their" words.

After connection, and coming out of that meditative state can sometimes lead to you feeling ungrounded so practice grounding exercises and do something that will bring you back into the here and now, for instance, take the dog for a walk sit in the garden with a cup of tea, prepare lunch or dinner.

Protection

Your Spirit Guide can be called upon to protect you. Remember my earlier words about protection: You can imagine you are in a bubble, a jam jar, or in a tube. Each day as you clean your teeth, morning and night, mentally ask your guide to be with you in your "bubble" to enhance your gift and protect you.

This is a good practice to get into. Your Guide will give that added protection to you. You just have to have the belief and trust that they are there keeping you safe

Often we ask the question of what our guides expect of us – we have to let go of expectation of all kinds to enable our guidance to encourage and lead to spiritual growth.

Our guides often hope rather than want or expect certain things to develop from a serious connection with them.

Many Spirit Guides are concerned to help us in these times, with healing, information, spiritual growth, teaching and the 'thinning of the veil' between the different other worlds and dimensions.

Your Guide may let you know that they have a certain area of interest, and this will often coincide with any special area of interest of your own.

Healers, for example often find that they develop a strong contact with a healing Guide, who will strengthen and focus their channeling of healing and support as well as their development of healing techniques, and may also pass on to them ways in which they can give further help to those who come to them for healing

The words channelled through Maurice Barbenell from Silver Birch have been written in many books and have been an inspiration to a number of people during their Spiritual Awakening. These are a few words on Spirit Guides which came through during a trance demonstration.

A question asked during the demonstration:

"I receive guidance, I am aware of it and the level from which it is coming.

I have not been able to know whether this is coming from a general source or a particular guide. Is there any way by which prayer or meditation can lead one to this knowledge?"

The reply was: *"Shall I repeat words that are very familiar? When the pupil is ready the master appears. Is that not the answer? Do not bother about it. All guidance streams from the Great Spirit. Ambassadors from the hierarchy and other enlightened beings, who are kindred souls as far as you are concerned, attach themselves to you sometimes before you are born into your world.*

Sometimes they make themselves known to you before you incarnate into your world; sometimes you agree with them that you will volunteer to perform certain tasks.
It does not matter what names you call them. They are there. They do not leave you. Their task is as it says in your Bible, "He shall give his angels charge concerning thee."

These are the angels of light who surround their charges, whose self-imposed task is to guard, to guide, to sustain them and always to point the way to the spiritual path that ultimately leads to mastery. It is not an easy path; it is strewn with rocks and boulders. It becomes increasingly difficult as familiar landmarks have to be left behind. But as correspondingly low as you sink, so you can rise, and the heights to which you can aspire are infinite. Perfection is not a process that you will attain. It is one which you will always be in the process of attaining. If you wish to gain the prizes of the spirit you must prepare to make sacrifices, but once attained they can never be lost

We are aware of all your difficulties, your problems and your desires. We know that you live in a material world.

We have access to the sources of supply to ensure that those who serve will never go hungry or thirsty. All that is necessary will be provided.

What we say to you and to everyone we encounter is to do the best you can; no more is expected of you. When you fall down you can pick yourself up".

These words give an insight to what the spirit world can tell us during a trance demonstration. Trance will be explained in more detail in a later book. These words by Silver Birch coming through trance were printed into a number of books available even now, so the spirit of Silver Birch speaks with such simplicity and truth and the words are still read today. This communication is wonderful proof that the inspiration we receive can be very profound.

The spirit world can only ask for us to do our best to work with love and light and not to expect too much of ourselves.

These words "when you fall down you can pick yourself up" take heed because you will need this encouragement during your journey.

It can sometimes be frustrating and demanding but, will always bring joy and fulfillment to you.

Chapter Three

Angelic Forces

The word Angel means Messenger. Angels are woven into our belief structure to do with religious concepts. They bring us light and laughter, as well as enabling our finite mind to arrive at a wider understanding of divinity, infinity and the scheme of the universe. Angels are eager to teach us about the nature of light and help us understand the dimension of levity as well as that of gravity.

Angels belong to a collective body, within which there is a mutual support and an evolutionary pattern. They emanate from the Divine Source and are divided into groups. Each group has a specific task or area of interest. Angels are beyond gender and fully balanced in masculine and feminine principle. There are three main angelic realms and each realm has three sub-divisions.

The angels which are said to be the closest to the divine energy are called **Heavenly Counsellors**. Their sub-divisions are:
Seraphim —the most evolved of the group, who work to keep balance and alignment between planets, stars and other heavenly bodies by working with sound.

Cherubim – who work as guardians of all the light and colour energy in the universe.

Thrones– are the angelic overseers of each planet. The earth throne also concerns itself with balances between species and endeavours to prevent or modify such disasters as major flooding, drought, earthquakes etc.

The next angelic realm is that of **Heavenly Governors**. The sub-divisions are as follows:

Dominions– are the counsellors, advisers, supporters and teachers of all evolving angels. They particularly assist each guardian angel in looking after the well being of the incarnate individual to whom they have been assigned.

Virtues– are the listeners, who respond to prayers and requests for healing.

Powers-are the inspirers of human consciousness or higher ideals who also oversee the rhythms of birth, death and rebirth.

The third angelic realm is the **Messengers**. The sub divisions are as follows:

Principalities-are the overseers and guardians of large groups and organisations, nations and cities.

Archangels-oversee all aspects of human endeavour and help us to name, interpret and work with higher qualities.

Archangels can be invoked to bring blessing, safety and protection into our daily lives, and to assist us in gaining greater clarity about our life's purposes. Mainly, it is the archangels who are given traditional and specific names

Gabriel means "The Divine is my strength" He is the guardian of the south, noon, summer and our emotions. His element is water and his colour is green. Gabriel is the angel of revelation and hope and healing to dysfunctional families.

Uriel means "The light and fire of the Divine" He is the guardian of the east, the rising sun, dawn, morning and spring. His element is fire and his colour yellow. Uriel blesses our minds and inspires the worlds of science, and politics. He urges us towards social equality and helps us to find our direction in life.

Raphael means "The Divine has healed". He is the guardian of the west, twilight, evening, autumn and healing. His element is earth and his colour is red. He blesses growth, transformation and all forms of healing, from surgery to herbalism and the "laying on of hands". He brings comfort and protection to all who are physically, spiritually or emotionally ill.

Michael: meaning "Who is like the Divine". He is guardian of the direction of the north, of night-time, of the season of winter, the element of air, spirits and dreams. His special colour is blue. He brings the blessings of co-operation, reconciliation and peace

Angels without other titles—these angels come closest to our earthly vibrations and bring us angelic qualities such as joy, laughter, harmony, peace, love, synchronicity and many others. In this sub-division are our Guardian Angels. Each time the soul decides to embark on the process of incarnation a guardian angel comes into being through the process of evolution. Therefore from before gestation to the journey into and beyond death each one of us is accompanied by an angelic presence, who without interfering with our freedom of choice will lovingly guide and protect us.

When we die, our guardian angels guide us throughout that great journey and only when we have completely adapted to life beyond do they move on to the next stage of their evolution or to another task within the angelic hierarchy.

Your guardian angel will always be with you throughout your present lifetime. This accompanying presence came into being at the moment at which your soul decided you would incarnate and was there at your conception and birth. Your guardian angel will be with you at your death and will accompany you through that transition until you are at peace in the realms of light.

It is not the angel's task to live our lives for us. Angels and guides will try to make themselves heard but if we are determined on a certain course, they cannot override us.

Only when we are in co-operation with them or with natural forces of harmony, can they steer us to live our lives to the fullest positive potential.

When human beings tread a dark or destructive path, they have cut themselves off from the light, which always lies just beyond the self-made or self-inflicted darkness. We must be careful not to opt out of responsibility for our actions and those of our fellow being. We must never take an over-simplistic view. It is often the experience of either personal or collective darkness which proves the greatest catalyst. We cannot have free choice and complete protection or rescue from the results

Angels are ever present allies, our connection with them can be evoked by learning to live with harmony of nature, fun, laughter. During our mundane everyday life, an angel is ever present. Bringing "Play and creativity" into our lives will enable us to be aware of this wonderful presence

Our Guides and Angels are an aspect of our guidance and evolving spiritual awareness. Let them guide you and be your friend – but remember they know you are living on this earth plane and will try to inspire you according to the laws of nature and the universe.

There is no such thing as coincidence, learn to watch where synchronicity begins to happen and allow yourself to go with the "flow" of things. I have a saying:

GO WITH FLO SHE'S A BIG GIRL

Chapter Six

Soul, Spirit and Higher Consciousness

To understand fully the concept of the difference between spirit and soul, we must first believe that the soul comes from the Source (the Divine Energy or God essence). In order to become like the Source and also ensure the Source is not static, the soul takes on incarnation and journeys through many lifetimes in search of evolution.

Gradually an overseeing, observing or higher self emerges and then each time incarnation takes place only a part of the whole becomes personified in order to undergo the further experience which the essence requires in its search for wholeness. When the soul thread is sufficiently evolved, the wheel of rebirth is no longer its main concern or focus.

There is then an opportunity to continue on the path of evolution of being of service in different ways. Guides and communicators have agreed to aid the collective journey by sharing the less finite view and wider perspective seen from other planes of being.

This is why guides seek individuals on earth with whom to communicate so that they can help in making the experience of incarnation less blinkered or limited in vision.

Guides cross the interface between planes in order to communicate. They have different concerns or aims in making their contact with incarnate human beings. For some, the main focus will be healing, for others, teaching, whilst yet others will seek to inspire the artist, poet, architect, musician or writer.

The Soul is the "whole", while the spirit is the thread or an essence or part of the whole. It can be likened to an orange, each section being part of the whole. As each section incarnates on this earth plane that is when we become that spirit entity to experience that incarnation.

The Soul also will belong to Soul groups, which to continue the analogy of the orange the group will belong to the same tree, growing together for the higher good but, will have individual oranges all evolving at different rates.

The complete being does not incarnate. The sections of each orange will have threads which are aspects of the essential soul. The number of sections in each orange will vary from soul to soul.

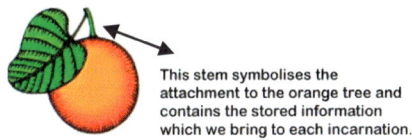

This stem symbolises the attachment to the orange tree and contains the stored information which we bring to each incarnation.

We are all aspects of MIND, SPIRIT AND SOUL As we gain in our experience, our higher mind, or consciousness will begin to retain the information for each lifetime incarnation.

The higher mind maintains the Auric field and will bring about if possible the purpose of this incarnation, so we are born knowing that purpose—it is as time goes on we need to strive to remember our reasons for being here this time.

Many people believe that it is the soul that incarnates, but most Spirit Guides teach us that is actually the spirit that illuminates, vitalises and is totally present within our incarnate beings, while the soul observes and oversees.

The higher self is an aspect of soul that carries and interprets the growing body of knowledge and wisdom that is acquired by living incarnate lives.

It organizes our pattern of incarnation and evolution and decides what kind of incarnation in needed or necessary for the continuation of our eternal learning process.

When we die, our spirit or essence returns to the soul stem or thread so that the learning from any given lifetime can be integrated with the learning experience from other lifetimes.

When our need for learning through incarnation is over soul and spirit are totally reunited. The image often given for this reunification is that of the chalice of the soul contains the flame of the spirit in the ultimate mystical marriage.

Karma and reincarnation or cause and effect has a bearing on life's journey.

I as I am now, and you as you are now, in this present lifetime, have never incarnated before and will never incarnate again

We are one of the segments from the orange connected to the tree by our soul stem. When we return to the soul stem, taking the experiences we have gathered in this life with us, another personality (another segment from the orange) will seek to broaden our incarnate experience.

Such a subsequent incarnating personality may also seek to continue work we have begun or redeem imbalances we have created and will seek to broaden the experience.

Such purposes or "menus" are created by our higher selves. Our Personal Spirit Guides are close to our higher selves and understand our higher overall purposes.

Guides and Angels help us to maintain a healthy balance between all aspects of our being. The Power Angels are keepers of the "akashic records". These records are the collective records of the souls evolutionary journey and I will tell you about these in Book Three.

It is thought that every human thought and action creates waves that will affect all other members of the human race, the Power Angels keep the collective recordings of all human kind.

It is a fact that thoughts provoke action because thoughts are a living entity of our mind, affecting our body and coming from the soul.

Look at the diagram on the following page it will make sense of how everything interacts with each other; MIND – SOUL – SPIRIT

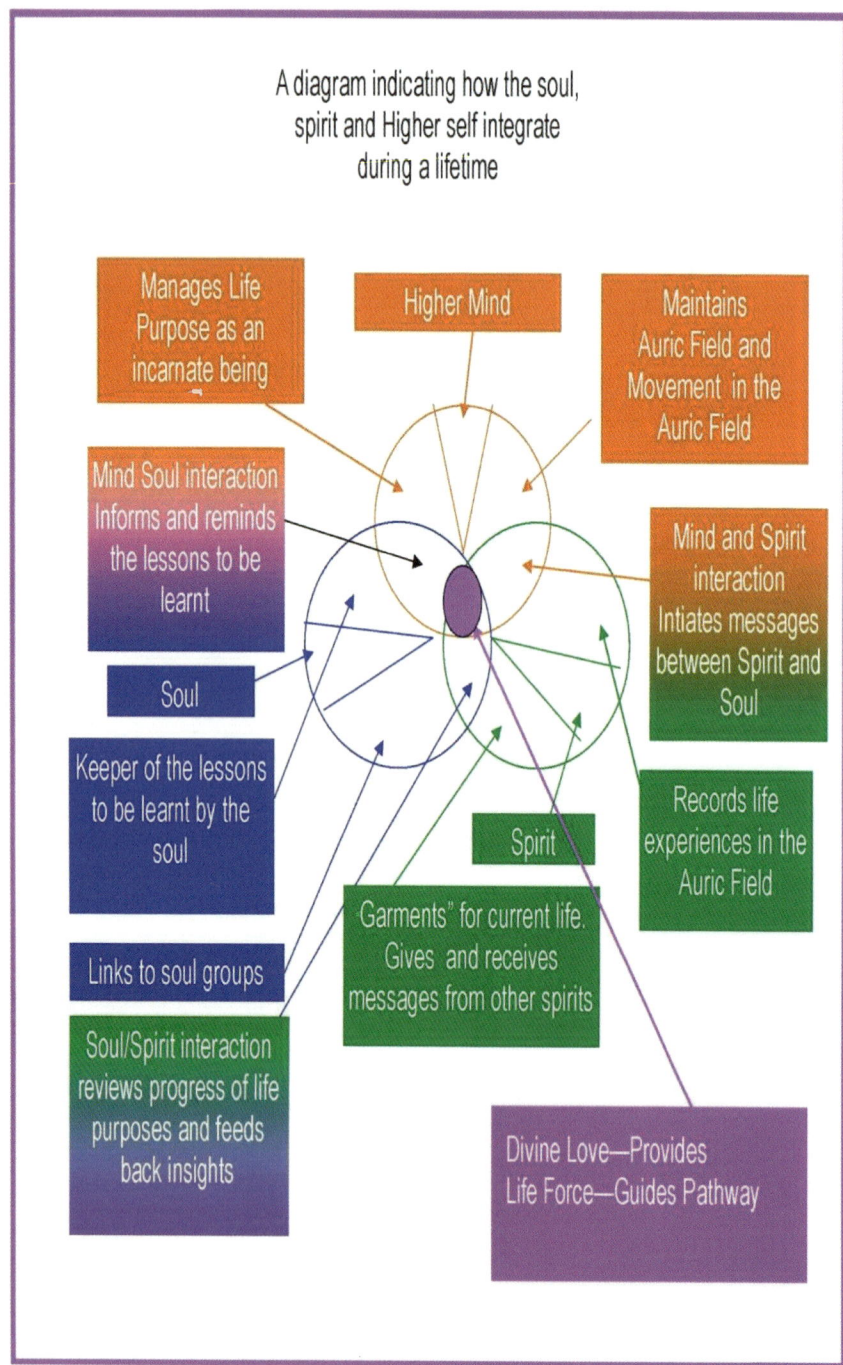

Understanding the links with our Guides and Angels can help maintain the link with the Spirit World. As our knowledge increases we can overcome the doubt of our ability. Reading these books you will gain information and understanding of the why's and wherefore's of spiritual awareness.

Nothing can prepare you for the wonderful journey you are beginning.

I want to describe a dream I had many years ago. In that dream I had been taken to attend a special meeting. My Uncle Sid and Auntie Elsie (both in the Spiritualist Movement at the time) beckoned me towards a huge table and sat me down. The room seemed enormous and echoed with voices and musical sounds. As I looked on the table a book was opened before me, Uncle Sid told me to sign, I was signing an important contract he told me. Somehow, I felt it was right and didn't question what I was being told. Behind the desk was a man dressed all in white with white hair, a long white beard. His eyes met mine as I put my signature on this book and he smiled. No words were exchanged.

When I awoke I recorded this dream in a little book beside my bed. At the time I thought little of this signpost. Because that is exactly what it was. My Uncle Sid had shown me I was signing up to serve Spirit, the man behind the desk has since revealed himself to me as a great philosopher guide who has worked with me for some time now. I laugh now because when I awoke from that dream it was so intense; I thought I had been in the presence of "GOD", it was in fact this very evolved Spirit Guide.

Look out for the dreams that are so vivid you will know the difference.

Always keep a notebook by the side of the bed so you can make a note of everythin; you will refer to this as time goes by and things will become clearer and the jigsaw will start to piece together.

Love and Light

Pam

BOOK THREE CONTAINS:

LAYERS OF THE AURIC FIELD
THE AKASHIC RECORDS
MENTAL MEDIUMSHIP – HEALING

Printed in Great Britain
by Amazon.co.uk, Ltd.,
Marston Gate.